WOMEN
ATHLETES
OF THE
2000
OLYMPICS

SUPERSTARS
of U.S.A. Women's Soccer

JOE LAYDEN

Aladdin Paperbacks

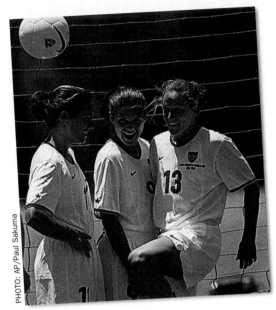

PHOTO: AP/Paul Sakuma

For Emily

EDITOR'S NOTE: The athletes featured in this book should form the core of the 2000 Summer Olympic team. However, this book was written and published several months before a final roster could be determined. Injuries, late changes, and the emergence of rising stars could affect the final roster. Our apologies if any athletes were overlooked.

First Aladdin Paperbacks edition August 2000

Text copyright © 2000 by Joe Layden

Designed by Michael Malone All interior photos courtesy of AP/Wide World Photos

Aladdin Paperbacks An imprint of Simon & Schuster Children's Publishing Division 1230 Avenue of the Americas New York, NY 10020

Printed and bound in the United States of America 10 9 8 7 6 5 4 3 2 1

Library of Congress Catalog Card Number 00-101198 ISBN 0-689-83593-0

FRONT COVER PHOTO: ALLSPORT/Ezra Shaw. BACK COVER PHOTO: AP/Beth A. Keiser

Let the Games Begin!

With a brilliant Southern California sun blazing overhead, the United States soccer team jogs back out onto the field at the Rose Bowl in Pasadena.

It's late in the afternoon on July 10, 1999, the final day of the Women's World Cup Soccer Tournament. For 120 minutes—through regulation and two overtime periods—the U.S. and China have played passionate, perfect soccer. Now, with the score tied 0–0, they will have to settle the issue with penalty kicks. As the teams line up for the final shoot-out, 90,185 spectators stand and fill the elegant, old stadium with a deafening roar. It's easily the largest crowd ever to see a women's soccer game. And 40 million more are watching anxiously at home on television. That's about the same number of viewers who typically tune in for the NBA Finals!

Kristine Lilly heads the ball as Brazil's Tania defends during the first half of their 1999 Women's World Cup semifinals game.

3

The spectacle of it all is almost overwhelming. Just a few short years ago, women's soccer was virtually ignored. Its best players could walk down the street unnoticed. Now, in the tense final moments of this championship game, the U.S. women's soccer team stands at the center of the athletic universe. As Kristine Lilly, America's tireless midfielder, will later say: "The World Cup showed that we can play great soccer and draw in the crowds. There are no excuses now. We're doing it, and we're right in you're face!"

There's no doubt about that. The U.S. women soccer players will be among the most visible athletes this year at the 2000 Summer Olympics in Sydney, Australia.

Most of the women who starred for the U.S. World Cup team will be back in uniform for the Olympics. Several of them, including Mia Hamm, Julie Foudy, and Michelle Akers, have played for the U.S. National Team for more than a decade. For them, the Sydney Games could represent the end of a long and remarkable journey. A journey that began quietly in 1991, with precious few people watching.

It was in the summer of that year that the United States won the very first Women's World Cup Soccer Tournament. Not that anyone really noticed. As Hamm recalls, "We won the tournament and you couldn't even find the result in the newspaper. Nobody cared."

The situation wasn't a whole lot different four years later, when the U.S. lost in overtime to Norway and finished third in the 1995 World Cup. Even then, for the most part, the women of U.S. soccer toiled in anonymity.

But that hardly dampened their enthusiasm. Unselfish, ambitious, and

Members of the U.S. Women's Soccer Team on a night out on the town. From left to right: Kate Sobrero, Danielle Fotopoulos, Sara Whalen, Mia Hamm, Julie Foudy, Christie Pearce, and Brandi Chastain.

Mia Hamm, surrounded by the media, as usual.

focused, they were a team in the truest sense of the word. They lived together, trained together, competed together. They supported each other in hard times and complimented each other in good times. And they were determined to be ambassadors for their sport. Unlike many professional athletes, the women of the U.S. National Team understood their roles—both on and off the field. Jealousy never got in the way of the team's common goal, and ego never stood between the players and their young fans. As they toured the country playing exhibition games and preparing for the 1996 Olympics, the U.S. women were always accessible, always quick with a smile and an autograph.

"When you see the look on the faces of these kids, especially the girls, it's just so uplifting," says Foudy. "We take our responsibility as role models very seriously."

The United States won the gold medal at the 1996 Olympics by beating China, 2–1, in the championship game. More than 76,000 fans filled the University of Georgia's Sanford Stadium for that game.

Afterward, during the medal ceremony, the U.S. players held hands and sang along with "The Star-Spangled Banner" as thousands of flashbulbs flickered and popped throughout the stadium. "It was awesome," Lilly remembers. "It was the kind of moment every athlete lives for."

She couldn't have known it then, but there would be more such moments for Lilly and her teammates—bigger and better moments.

In the months leading up to the 1999 Women's World Cup, which would be hosted by the United States, Soccer Mania gripped the country. It helped, of course, that soccer had already become the most popular participatory sport in the U.S. More than seven million women and girls were playing the game—from youth leagues to Division I college programs, to adult recreation leagues, women's soccer was booming!

And, not surprisingly, the stars of the U.S. National Team were losing their grip on obscurity. Mia Hamm was the first to break out—a striking striker who was not only the best soccer player in the world,

Back-up goalie Saskia Webber, sporting a stars and stripes hairdo.

PHOTO: AP/Elise Amendola

but also (according to *People* magazine) one of the 50 Most Beautiful People in the world. And one of the athletes most coveted by advertisers, pitching for Barbie one day and Gatorade the next. But Mia wasn't alone. Kristine Lilly was also featured in a national advertising campaign, and Julie Foudy received critical acclaim for her broadcasting work.

As the team toured and competed in a series of exhibitions to prepare for the World Cup, people took notice. The crowds began to swell. Everywhere they went, the women of U.S. soccer were mobbed by adoring fans. It was exhausting, but they didn't mind in the least.

"When we were kids, we didn't have women soccer players to look up to," says defender Brandi Chastain. "That's why everyone on this team is so accessible."

Their patience and persistence were rewarded during the World Cup. Sellout crowds screamed themselves hoarse each time the U.S. played, from a 3–0 opening-day win over Norway through the final

moments of the championship game against China.

Two images from that day burn brightest. The first is goalie Briana Scurry diving to her left to stop a penalty kick by China's Liu Ying. The second is Brandi Chastain falling to her knees and ripping off her jersey in sheer exultation after her penalty kick had given the U.S. a 5–4 shootout victory.

With her fists held high, and the screams of more than 90,000 delirious fans raining down on her, Chastain knelt alone on the Rose Bowl turf for only a moment. Soon she was engulfed by her teammates. The World Cup champs rolled in a pack across the field, hugging and laughing and crying.

"We didn't want to lose the Cup again," Chastain said afterward. "We wanted to regain it for the pride of our team, for the pride of our country, for the pride of U.S. soccer."

They accomplished all of that...and more. In the weeks that followed, the members of the U.S. National Team became genuine celebrities. President Clinton, who attended the championship game with his daughter Chelsea, thanked the team "for the gift you have given the United States." They were honored with a parade at Disneyland. They chatted with David Letterman and Jay Leno.

Soon, though, the team was back at work. The job, you see, is not quite finished. For Mia Hamm, Julie Foudy, Briana Scurry, Kristine Lilly, Brandi Chastain, Carla Overbeck, Michelle Akers...and all the other women of the U.S. National Team, there is one more goal to attain: a gold medal in Sydney!

Pure jubilation, as Brandi Chastain is engulfed by teammates Shannon MacMillan (8), Sara Whalen (7), and Kate Sobrero (20), after kicking the game-winning overtime penalty shootout kick against China during the World Cup Final at the Rose Bowl in Pasadena, California.

PHOTO: AP/Elise Amendola

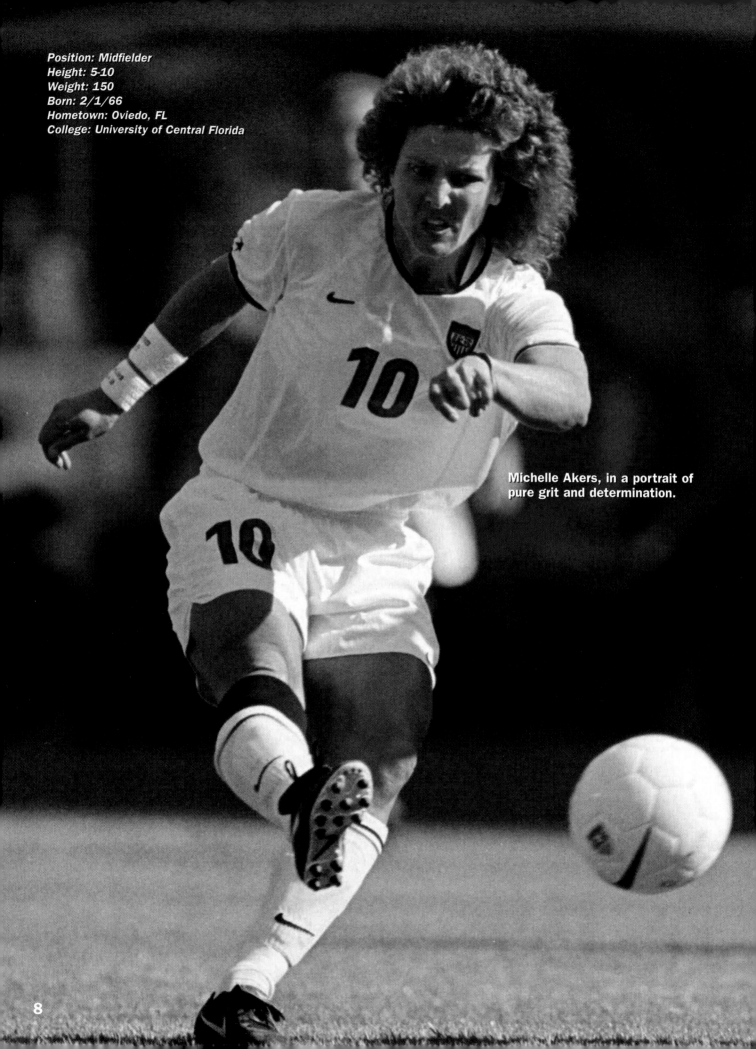

Position: Midfielder
Height: 5-10
Weight: 150
Born: 2/1/66
Hometown: Oviedo, FL
College: University of Central Florida

Michelle Akers, in a portrait of pure grit and determination.

Michelle Akers

Michelle is helped off the field after taking a hard hit in the 1999 World Cup Final against China.

Because of her long, flowing mane, Michelle Akers' teammates have given her the nickname Mufasa, after the noble character in the Disney animated film *The Lion King*. But that's not the only reason it's appropriate. You see, the oldest member of the U.S. team is also its most courageous.

For the past decade Michelle has suffered from a debilitating disease known as chronic fatigue syndrome. She has tried to control the disease by being careful with her diet, but sometimes it has left her so weak that she can barely stand up, let alone play soccer. At the 1996 Summer Olympics in Atlanta, for instance, Michelle had to take fluids intravenously after every game. She was terribly sick. But she kept playing, and she was instrumental in helping the U.S. win a gold medal.

"Michelle is the heart of this team," Mia Hamm says. "Her being out there gives us so much."

In the past, Michelle was primarily an offensive player. At the first Women's World Cup in 1991, she scored a tournament-best 10 goals to lead the U.S. to the championship. More recently, though, Michelle has moved to midfield, where her intelligence and experience are a huge asset. And as she proved during the 1999 World Cup, Michelle has lost none of her heart. In the final moments of the shootout against China, Michelle was in the locker room, an IV needle inserted into each arm, and an oxygen mask on her face. In addition to being severely dehydrated, she had suffered a concussion after colliding with goalkeeper Briana Scurry near the end of regulation.

But when Brandi Chastain's winning kick settled into the back of the net, Michelle sat up, removed her IV lines, and staggered out onto the field to join the celebration.

"Knowing that I gave the team every ounce of effort I could muster was very satisfying for me," Michelle later told fans on her internet Web site. "I simply left everything I had on the field."

Brandi Chastain

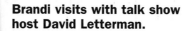

PHOTO: AP/Patrick D. Pagnano

Brandi visits with talk show host David Letterman.

With one swift kick, followed by a wild celebration, Brandi Chastain secured her place in history. It was her goal that gave the United States a dramatic shootout victory over China in the championship game of the 1999 Women's World Cup.

A decade ago, Brandi hardly seemed destined to become an American hero. Afer being named Freshman Player of the Year at the University of California, Berkeley, she suffered a series of devastating injuries. After enduring reconstructive surgery on both of her knees, Brandi transferred to Santa Clara University, where she slowly began rebuilding her career. She hadn't played in two full years, and a lot of people questioned whether she would ever regain her form. But they had no idea just how tough Brandi was.

After getting cut from the U.S. National Team in 1993, Brandi was invited to try out again in 1995. There was, however, a catch. The team's new coach, Tony DiCicco, wanted Brandi to switch from offense to defense. Brandi wasn't fazed. Even though she had been a forward her entire career, she accepted her new role. And she made the team! She played every minute of the United States' five games during the 1996 Olympics, and helped the team win a gold medal.

Brandi is also a fierce competitor who thrives under pressure, which was never more evident than in last summer's World Cup shootout against China. She took the final, game-clinching shot for the U.S. When the ball sailed cleanly into the back of the net, she ripped off her shirt and dropped to her knees in a display of pure joy. Then she was mobbed by her teammates.

"To me (taking off my shirt) symbolized shedding the weight of the whole tournament," Brandi says. "It was like taking a big sigh of relief and saying, 'We did it! We won!'"

PHOTO: AP/Michael Caulfield

Brandi clears the ball during the first period of overtime in the World Cup Final against China.

CHASTAIN

Position: *Defender*
Height: *5-7*
Weight: *130*
Born: *7/21/68*
Hometown: *San Jose, CA*
College: *Santa Clara University*

Joy Fawcett

It was in the fall of 1997 when Joy Fawcett earned the title of World's Ultimate Soccer Mom. Joy was raising two small children at the time. She was coaching a youth club team and the UCLA women's team. Oh…and in her spare time? She was a standout defender for the U.S. National Team.

By the end of the year Joy had given up the coaching jobs to concentrate on preparing for the Women's World Cup. But she never cut back on her duties as a mother. Joy's two little girls, Katelyn and Carli, became temporary members of the U.S. contingent. They traveled all over the world with their mom. While most of her teammates stuffed their duffle bags with shin guards and cleats, Joy had to remember to pack diapers and toys and baby food. Sometimes she was exhausted before she even stepped on the field. But she never complained, and she never slowed down.

"If anything," teammate Shannon MacMillan said of Joy before the World Cup, "she's gotten better."

That's saying a lot, considering how much Joy had already accomplished. A three-time All-American at the University of California, Berkeley, she was a member of the United States' World Cup championship team in 1991, and the Olympic gold medal-winning team in 1996. Joy has been playing soccer since she was five years old. She's one of the oldest players on the U.S. squad, but she insists she loves the game as much now as she did when she was a child. Maybe that's why her nickname is Joyful.

Joy raises her hands after scoring a goal during the quarterfinal match against Germany in the 1999 World Cup.

Joy fires a shot on goal against China in the 1999 World Cup Final.

PHOTO: AP/Kevork Djansezian

Position: Defender
Height: 5-5
Weight: 130
Born: 2/8/68
Hometown: Huntington Beach, CA
College: University of California, Berkeley

PHOTO: AP/Robert Borea

Position: Midfielder
Height: 5-6
Weight: 130
Born: 1/23/71
Hometown: Mission Viejo, CA
College: Stanford University

Julie Foudy

From left to right: Mia Hamm, Cindy Parlow, Julie Foudy, and Carla Overbeck.

PHOTO: AP/John Gress

Julie Foudy is the unofficial goodwill ambassador for the sport of women's soccer. She's smart, funny, and charming. And she's never too busy to sign an autograph for a young fan.

"There's nothing like seeing that look on a little girl's face," Julie says. "They're thinking, 'Wow! If she can play soccer for the U.S., maybe I can, too.'"

Julie is so charismatic that it's sometimes easy to forget about her athletic ability. You see, the most outgoing member of the U.S. team is also one of its best players. A four-time All-American at Stanford, Julie was just 20 years old when she helped the U.S. win the first Women's World Cup in 1991. She also was a member of the 1996 Olympic championship team.

Julie's love for soccer is clear. She graduated from Stanford with a degree in biology and was accepted into medical school. But she repeatedly postponed her medical career so that she could continue to compete on the soccer field. She enjoys the game so much that she even works as a television commentator for both men's and women's soccer games. Julie received high praise for her work during the 1998 Men's World Cup, and she has since decided that her future might be in broadcasting, rather than medicine.

"There are so many things I want to do," Julie says.

First on the list, of course, is helping the U.S. win another gold medal in Sydney.

PHOTO: AP/Elise Amendola

Julie battles for the ball against Ireland in an exhibition game in 1999.

Mia Hamm

Position: Forward
Height: 5-5
Weight: 130
Born: 3/17/72
Hometown: Chapel Hill, NC
College: University of North Carolina

A ferocious attacke[r] Mia takes a shot or goal against Finlan[d]

PHOTO: AP/Ed Zurga

The most famous female soccer player in the world is camera-shy. Really. Despite all of the television commercials and endorsements, Mia Hamm really doesn't like publicity.

"I accept it because it's good for the sport," she says. "But I don't particularly like to talk about myself, mainly because I don't want to believe my own press. There's still so much I need to do, so many things I've yet to accomplish. I have a lot of responsibilities to a lot of people—my teammates and my family—and I want to keep that as the most important thing for me, not how many magazines I get in or how many commercials I do."

Mia already has acquired a lifetime of notable accomplishments. She's been an Olympic gold medalist, World Cup champion, three-time All-American, and,

when she was only fifteen, she was the youngest player ever to make the U.S. National Team. With blazing speed and incomparable ball-handling skills, Mia is a threat every time she touches the ball.

"She has great acceleration and explosive abilities," says Mia's former coach on the national team, Tony DiCicco. "She's the whole package. She's exciting to watch. When Mia is on her game, there's not much argument that she's the best player in the world."

As the daughter of an Air Force officer, Mia moved around a lot when she was a child. She found that playing soccer helped her make friends quickly whenever she settled in a new town. She also discovered that sports boosted her self-confidence. When she conducts clinics for children—especially girls—she never hesitates to pass that message along.

"I want girls to understand the value of sports," Mia says. "Playing sports can give you a healthy mind and body. It can give you self-esteem and positively affect your relationships, and the way you approach your studies. Yes, it is just a game and you should always understand that. But also understand that it really makes you feel good about myself to go out there and compete and help your team try to win."

PHOTO: AP/Beth A. Keiser

At home alone: Mia stretches before practice.

Fiercely determined, Kristine pushes her way past a player for Denmark to gain control of the ball.

Position: *Midfielder*
Height: *5-4*
Weight: *130*
Born: *7/22/71*
Hometown: *Wilton, CT*
College: *University of North Carolina*

Kristine Lilly

Kristine Lilly is the most versatile member of the U.S. National Team. In thirteen years of international competition, she has played every position except goalkeeper. And in the 1999 Women's World Cup, she proved she could handle that role as well. When a header sailed passed goalie Briana Scurry in overtime of the championship game against China, the United States appeared to have run out of luck. Suddenly, though, there was Kristine, leaping in front of the net and using her head to deflect the ball away.

It was perhaps the most important play of the entire tournament. But, typically modest, Kristine downplayed its significance. "I was just doing my job," she said.

Regardless of the assignment, Kristine attacks her job passionately. A four-time All-American at the University of North Carolina, she is the fittest player on the U.S. squad, thanks to a brutal year-round training routine. That devotion pays off at game time, when Kristine becomes the Energizer Bunny (as her teammates sometimes call her). She keeps going and going and going.

"Usually, if you're incredibly fast, you can't run for very long, and if you can run all day, you're not very fast," UNC coach Anson Dorrance once told *Sports Illustrated*. "But Kristine is one of the fastest players on the field, and she can run all day."

Kristine stretches with teammate Carla Overbeck during practice before the 1999 Women's World Cup Final.

PHOTO: AP/Nick Ut

Position: Forward
Height: 5-2
Weight: 130
Born: 10/23/72
Hometown: Portland, OR
College: University of Portland

Tiffeny Milbrett

PHOTO: AP/Joe Cavaretta

Tiffeny jumps in the air after scoring the game-winning goal against China to win the gold medal at the 1996 Olympics.

When Tiffeny Milbrett was a little girl growing up in Portland, Oregon, she dreamed of becoming a famous actress and seeing her name in lights. She's had to settle for being a different kind of performer. But there's no denying that she's a star.

For a long time Tiffeny didn't have to stray far from home to be recognized for her talent. A two-time *Parade* magazine high school All-American, she decided to play college soccer in her backyard, at the University of Portland. She was a prolific offensive player who graduated as the school's all-time leading scorer. She even led the nation in scoring when she was a senior!

Tiffeny's uncanny ability to put the ball in the net came in handy when the U.S. played China in the championship game of the 1996 Summer Olympics. She scored the game-winning goal to give the U.S. the first gold medal in the history of Olympic women's soccer.

"I've always been a scorer," Tiffeny says. "Even when I was very little, all I wanted to do was get that ball, go down the field, go for the goal, and put it in the back of the net."

PHOTO: AP/Susan Ragan

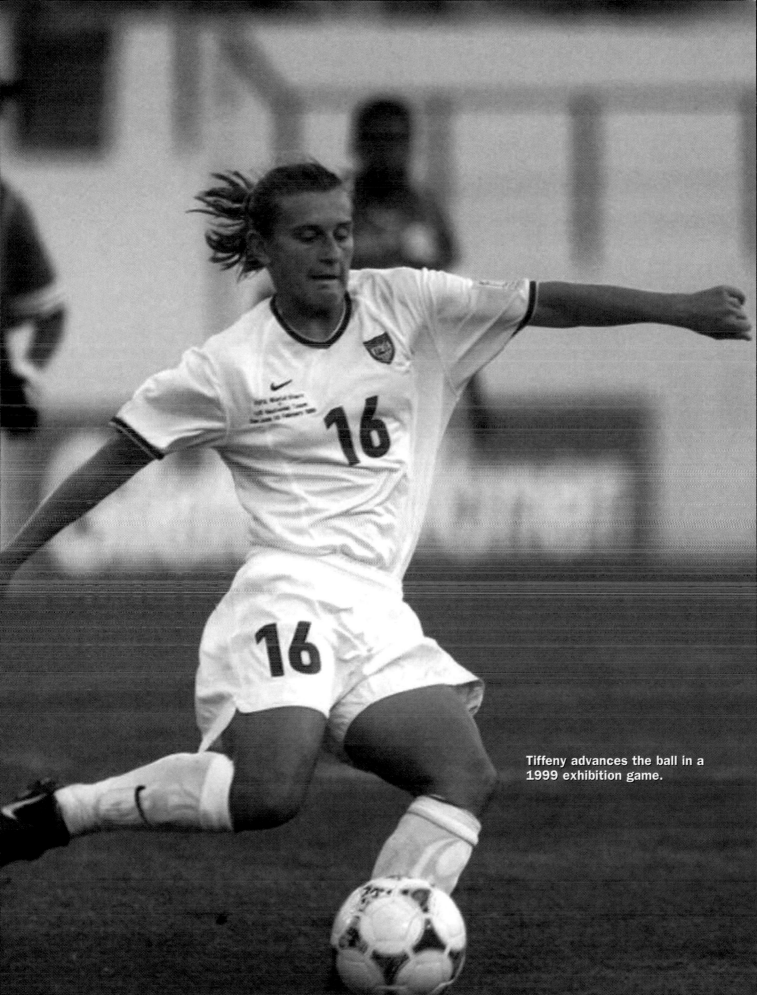

Tiffeny advances the ball in a 1999 exhibition game.

Position: Defender
Height: 5-7
Weight: 125
Born: 5/9/68
Hometown: Dallas, TX
College: University of
North Carolina

Carla Overbeck

You might think that Carla Overbeck would have a difficult time choosing the biggest moment in her life. Being named captain of the U.S. Olympic team in 1996? Winning a gold medal that same year? Helping the U.S. capture the World Cup last summer? Those are highlights, for sure, but they pale in comparison to the birth of Carla's son, Jackson, in 1997. As Carla says, the biggest thrill of her life now is "being a mom."

Although Carla's life has obviously changed significantly off the field, she remains as focused and intense as ever when she puts on a uniform. Some people, of course, wondered whether Carla's role as a mother would affect her play. But it hasn't. As teammate Julie Foudy says, "She's probably playing better than ever."

Carla is one of the steadiest and most reliable players in the history of U.S. soccer. She has not missed an international game since 1993, the longest streak of any U.S. player—male or female. No wonder Carla is often referred to as the Cal Ripken of U.S. soccer. She's a true ironwoman!

PHOTO: AP/Eric Risberg

Carla heads the ball during the 1999 Women's World Cup Final against China.

PHOTO: AP/Michael Caulfield

The moment she'd worked so hard for: Captain Carla Overbeck raises the trophy after defeating China for the World Cup Championship.

Position: Forward
Height: 5-11
Weight: 145
Born: 5/8/78
Hometown: Memphis, TN
College: University of North Carolina

Cindy
Parlow

Cindy beats her Nigerian opponent to the ball during the 1999 Women's World Cup.

PHOTO: AP/Beth A. Keiser

Cindy pushes the ball past the Brazilian goalie during the semifinal game of the 1999 Women's World Cup.

PHOTO: AP/Paul Sakuma

"I'm the chillin' type," Cindy Parlow insists. "I like to stay cool and calm."

For someone who believes patience and control are the most important parts of her game, Cindy sure moves quickly. As a baby, she learned how to walk by kicking and chasing a soccer ball around the house. Later, she was a straight-A student who graduated from high school in just three years. By the time she was 17 years old she was on the U.S. National team, and in 1996, at the age of 18, she became the youngest soccer player in history to win an Olympic gold medal.

A tireless player with an uncanny ability to find the net, Cindy is unde-niably one of the rising stars on the U.S. squad. Playing against Brazil in 1996, in front of some of the tough-est and loudest fans in the world, she scored two goals in her very first international game. With that per-formance Cindy let it be known that her youth was no barrier to success. That fall Cindy returned to the University of North Carolina and led the Tar Heels to the NCAA champi-onship. By the time she graduated, Cindy had twice won both the Hermann Trophy and Missouri Athletic Club Player of the Year award. The only other player to achieve that feat is Mia Hamm.

Obviously, Cindy is in pretty fast company. So what else is new?

Briana Scurry

Position: Goalkeeper
Height: 5-8
Weight: 145
Born: 9/7/71
Hometown: Dayton, MN
College: University of Massachusetts

A goalkeeper needs strong hands and a strong heart. Fortunately, Briana Scurry has both. She's a gifted athlete and a fearless competitor. There's nothing she likes better than facing an opponent one-on-one, even though it's the most difficult play for a goalie. As U.S. coach Tony DiCicco said after watching Briana make a brilliant save on a penalty kick during the World Cup shootout against China, "She has ice water in her veins."

Maybe that's because she grew up in the chilly town of Dayton, Minnesota, where hockey rinks far outnumber soccer fields. Briana actually liked hockey and wanted to give the sport a try, but her mother wouldn't allow it. She felt it was too dangerous. So, from the time she was 12 years old, Briana concentrated on basketball and, especially, soccer.

That turned out to be the right decision. A high school All-American, Briana landed a scholarship to the University of Massachusetts and led the Minutemen to the semifinals of the NCAA Tournament in 1993. She became the United States' top goalkeeper in 1994, and was in the net for every minute of the team's gold-medal run during the 1996 Olympics.

Briana was the only African-American starter on the U.S. World Cup team. She'd like to use her visibility to help make soccer more popular in America's inner cities, as well as the suburbs. Adding another Olympic gold medal to her trophy case would help in that mission, of course.

"Being an African-American soccer player is not so much a weight that I carry," Briana says. "It's more like a banner."

PHOTO: AP/Luca Bruno

PHOTO: AP/Eric Risberg

Briana blocks the penalty shot that enables the U.S. to take the 1999 Women's World Cup.

Briana exults during the gold medal ceremony at the 1996 Summer Olympics. The U.S. beat China 2–1 to win the first ever medal awarded in women's soccer at an Olympic Games.

Position: Defender
Height: 5-9
Weight: 140
Born: 8/23/76
Hometown: Bloomfield Hills, MI
College: Notre Dame

Kate battles for the ball during World Cup soccer action in Chicago. The USA defeated Nigeria 7–1.

Kate Sobrero

Off the field, Kate Sobrero seems like the nicest person you'd ever want to meet. Put her in a soccer uniform and a strange transformation takes place. Kate becomes a ferociously competitive young woman who will do almost anything to keep the ball out of her zone. How tough is Kate? Well…just decide for yourself.

During a practice in January of 1998 she collided with goalkeeper Tracy Ducar and sustained a fractured jaw. In order to heal properly, Kate's jaw had to be wired shut for six weeks. Somehow, though, Kate made her debut for the U.S. National Team in April. By May she was in the starting lineup.

"Kate is one of the best defenders in the world," says former U.S. coach Tony DiCicco. "And she's going to keep getting better and better."

Defenders don't always get as much recognition as offensive players, but Kate doesn't mind. She was the Defensive MVP of the 1995 NCAA Tournament, in which she led Notre Dame to the cham-

Kate plays tough defense even during practice drills.

pionship. And she still takes great pride in stopping her opponent.

"I love defense," Kate says. "Sliding around, taking the ball away from people…it's great. I get a thrill out of shutting someone down. I love to get them frustrated and watch them get all mad. Defense is my thing."

PHOTO: AP/Kathy Willens

Danielle
Fotopoulos
Forward

A prolific offensive player, Danielle holds the NCAA record for career goals. She found the net 118 times during her four years at the University of Florida. The most memorable of her goals unquestionably came in 1998, when she scored the game-winner in the NCAA championship. Danielle is perhaps the best all-around athlete on the team. In addition to being the best soccer player at Lyman High School in Longwood, Fla., she was a conference champion in tennis, led her basketball and cross country teams to state championships, and was named all-state in swimming. She also lettered in track and field.

Shannon
MacMillan
Forward

Shannon will always be remembered for her "golden goal"—an overtime goal against Norway in the semifinals of the 1996 Summer Olympics that propelled the U.S. into the gold-medal game against China. Not bad for a player who was originally cut from the pre-Olympic training roster and was forced to play her way back onto the team. But that's Shannon—she never quits! Shannon graduated from the University of Portland and was the 1995 National Player of the Year.

PHOTO: AP/Michael Lipchitz

PHOTO: AP/Steven Senne

Tisha
Venturini
Midfielder

A three-time All-American from the University of North Carolina, Tisha is a tireless worker who can score and play defense. She was second on the team in minutes played at the 1995 World Cup, and was tied for the team lead in goals scored. Tisha is also one of the toughest players in women's soccer. When she was at North Carolina, she recovered from a broken foot in only three weeks, just in time to win the MVP Award at the Atlantic Coast Conference Tournament.

Sara
Whalen
Defender

There isn't much Sara can't do on the soccer field. She switched from defense to offense in her senior year at the University of Connecticut and immediately became one of the top scorers in college soccer. Sara scored five goals in the NCAA playoffs in 1998 and led UConn all the way to the championship game. A three-time All-American, and the 1997 Soccer America Player of the Year, she'll be counted on to make a key contribution during the Olympics.

PHOTO: AP/Ed Zurga

Go Team USA!